Original title:
When I Knew

Copyright © 2024 Swan Charm
All rights reserved.

Author: Daisy Dewi
ISBN HARDBACK: 978-9916-89-655-6
ISBN PAPERBACK: 978-9916-89-656-3
ISBN EBOOK: 978-9916-89-657-0

The Dawn of Enlightenment

Awake, the light begins to rise,
In shadows past, new thought will thrive.
A whisper stirs the silent skies,
Illuminating minds alive.

With every dawn, old chains unbind,
The quest for truth, we boldly chase.
In clarity, the heart will find,
A pathway forged through time and space.

Pieces Falling into Place

Fragments scattered, lost and stray,
But slowly they begin to blend.
A jigsaw puzzle finds its way,
In chaos, harmony can mend.

Each moment spent, each choice we make,
Are threads of fate we soon will trace.
In twilight's glow, the scene will break,
Revealing grace in every place.

A Radiant Awakening

From slumber deep, the spirit stirs,
A spark ignites, igniting fire.
With fervent heart, our vision purrs,
Desire blooms, rising ever higher.

The world anew unfolds its grace,
Each step we take, our truth we find.
In beauty's mirror, we embrace,
The radiant light that warms the blind.

Echoes of Forgotten Knowledge

Whispers linger in the air,
Tales of wisdom lost in time.
In echoes soft, we hear the care,
Of ancestors who dared to climb.

Through ancient texts and sacred scrolls,
The past reveals its hidden keys.
To navigate our boundless souls,
And find the path of quiet ease.

Surrendering to Revelation

In shadows deep, the truth does hide,
A whisper calls, a gentle guide.
With open hearts, we dare to see,
The mysteries hidden, set us free.

Through lessons learned and tears once shed,
We find the paths our souls have tread.
With every heartbeat, wisdom grows,
In quiet moments, revelation flows.

In the Silence of Discovery

In stillness, echoes weave a tale,
Where thoughts drift free, like boats set sail.
A world unfolds in quiet grace,
Each hidden truth, a warm embrace.

The rustling leaves, a soft refrain,
Invite the heart to dance again.
In silent hours, light breaks the night,
Revealing wonders, pure delight.

The Key to Untold Stories

A key is forged in fire and time,
Unlocking doors to worlds sublime.
Each whispered thought, a tale to weave,
In every heart, a dream believes.

With pages turned and voices shared,
The stories bloom, no longer scared.
In every silence, echoes call,
The truth in stories waits for all.

A Sudden Shift in Perspective

In moments brief, the clouds may part,
Revealing colors, igniting heart.
A shift of view, a brand new sight,
Transforms the shadows into light.

What once was lost, now clear as day,
A new path forged in disarray.
In every challenge, wisdom grows,
A sudden change, the spirit knows.

Embers of Truth Ignited

In the quiet dark we see,
Flickers of a hidden flame.
Truth breaks the silence softly,
Igniting hearts, sparking name.

With every ember, wisdom blooms,
Illuminating the night's dread.
Shadows dance in light's whir,
As doubts and fears begin to shed.

Through the ashes, hope does rise,
Warming souls in cold despair.
A whisper rises to the skies,
Carrying truths beyond compare.

Against the Canvas of Illusion

Colors clash against the gray,
Dancing lights deceive our sight.
Brushstrokes woven in dismay,
Create a world both wrong and right.

Layers thick with dreams undone,
Mask the beauty lurking near.
Yet beneath, the threads are spun,
Whispers that the heart can hear.

Painted masks may hide the face,
Yet the essence shines so bright.
Finding truth in the embrace,
Of shadows dancing with the light.

Fragments of a Larger Whole

Pieces scatter in the wind,
Lost stories searching for their place.
Every shard has life within,
Contributing to time and space.

Each reflection tells a tale,
Merging paths of light and dark.
Together they will not fail,
Creating harmony's sweet spark.

In the chaos lies a thread,
Connecting all the hearts we share.
Through the cracks, new dreams are bred,
Whispers of hope fill the air.

The Revelation Beneath the Surface

Ripples dance upon the deep,
Secrets lie beneath the waves.
Veils of chance are what we keep,
As we search for hidden caves.

Every current tells a story,
Binding souls with unseen grace.
In the dark, there lies a glory,
A revelation we embrace.

Quiet waters harbor truth,
Gently pulling us to dive.
In the depths of ageless youth,
We discover how to thrive.

The Light Became Clear

In shadows deep, I wandered lost,
No guiding stars, I paid the cost.
But then a gleam broke through the night,
A promise shone, my heart took flight.

With every step, the path revealed,
A radiant truth, my wounds healed.
The doubt that bound my weary soul,
In dawning light, became my goal.

The fog recedes, the world awakes,
In brilliance new, my spirit shakes.
Each moment now, I stand and see,
A vibrant dream, I am set free.

In That Quiet Whisper

Among the noise, I sought a sound,
A soft embrace where peace is found.
In currents calm, I'd pause and pray,
The inner voice would guide my way.

A gentle nudge, a fleeting thought,
In silence deep, a truth was caught.
It spoke of love, of hope now near,
In whispered tones, I learned to hear.

The chaos fades, the heart complies,
In stillness vast, my spirit flies.
With every breath, I trust the spark,
A soothing balm dispels the dark.

A New Understanding

Through trials faced, the lessons learned,
In every twist, my spirit turned.
The journey long, yet worth the climb,
I found my voice, embraced the time.

With open heart, I faced the truth,
In moments raw, reclaimed my youth.
The veil was lifted, sight restored,
In wisdom gained, my soul adored.

Connection forged, I walked with grace,
Each step a dance, a warm embrace.
In unity, we all belong,
The world transformed, a vibrant song.

The Turning Point

When shadows cast, I felt the strain,
A heavy weight, a silent pain.
But deep inside, a spark ignites,
A chance to change, to seek new heights.

With trembling hands, I turned the page,
In courage found, embraced the stage.
The path ahead was bold and bright,
A thrilling journey, bathed in light.

In every trial, I gained my strength,
The turning point, a shift in length.
With open arms, I faced the dawn,
Renewed with hope, I moved along.

An Unseen Path Revealed

A whisper in the night,
Guides footsteps on the ground.
Shadows dance with light,
In silence, truths are found.

Through tangled roots we tread,
With hope as our lantern.
The heart knows where it's led,
Embracing the uncertain.

Each twist, a chance to grow,
A lesson in the strife.
In the wild, we learn to flow,
As we seek out new life.

Stars align with grace,
Illuminating the way.
In this sacred space,
Dawn breaks the night's dismay.

A journey, though unknown,
Leaves footprints in the sand.
The unseen paths we've grown,
Are shaped by gentle hands.

Among the Stars of Understanding

In a sky vast and bright,
Questions drift like the breeze.
Searching for what's right,
Hearts open, eager to seize.

Wisdom shines like a star,
Guiding us through the dark.
Each light, a sign from afar,
Illuminates reason's spark.

Together we explore,
The cosmos of the mind.
With each story we bore,
More truths we hope to find.

In the quiet we learn,
That knowledge is a flame.
With every page we turn,
Life's essence we proclaim.

Among these stars we stand,
United, strong, and free.
In the vastness, hand in hand,
We weave a tapestry.

The Canvas of Clarity

Strokes of light and shade,
Each hue a story told.
In colors we have made,
The memories we hold.

Brush meets canvas anew,
Transforming what we see.
Creating a view,
Of what we wish to be.

Mistakes blend into art,
Lessons painted in time.
Each canvas, where we start,
Becomes our own sublime.

With every splash, there's grace,
An expression of the soul.
In this sacred space,
Art makes the spirit whole.

From chaos, calm is born,
In beauty's warm embrace.
The world is soon adorned,
With clarity's soft trace.

Beneath the Surface

Rippling waters conceal,
The secrets held within.
Glimmers of what is real,
Lurking where dreams begin.

Dive into the unknown,
Past shadows and disguise.
Where truth has gently grown,
And wisdom never lies.

Voices from the deep,
Call out with silent grace.
In the stillness, we leap,
To uncover life's embrace.

Bubbles rise like thoughts,
A dance in tranquil pools.
The mind untangles knots,
As the heart gently rules.

Beneath the surface waits,
A story yet to bloom.
Courage, the key that gates,
The treasures in the gloom.

Awakening a Slumbering Heart

A whisper stirs the quiet night,
Gentle breezes, soft and light.
Dreams of old begin to rise,
In the darkness, hope replies.

Light breaks through the morning haze,
Unraveled threads of past's warm gaze.
Softly coursing, life returns,
A slumbering heart, it brightly burns.

Each petal blooms with colors bold,
Stories of the heart retold.
Awakened now, it beats with grace,
In rhythm with the world's embrace.

Through shadows cast by doubt and fear,
The melody of love draws near.
With every pulse, a vow is made,
A journey fresh, at dawn's cascade.

So let the heart reclaim its song,
In joyous notes, where it belongs.
For every beat is life anew,
Awakening the world in view.

Trails of Forgotten Wisdom

In silence echoes tales of old,
Ancient whispers yet untold.
Paths of wisdom, worn and clear,
Guide the hearts that wish to steer.

Leaves that flutter, breeze that sighs,
Wear the truths of earth and skies.
Each step taken, roots entwined,
In nature's arms, the soul aligned.

Through meadows green and mountains high,
The lessons flow, like rivers nigh.
Seek the secrets in the stream,
Where past and present softly dream.

The stones beneath, a story carved,
In every crack, a life unstarved.
The journey winds, with grace combined,
In trails of wisdom, love defined.

So gather 'round and share the lore,
For knowledge blooms forevermore.
In every heart, a spark still glows,
The wisdom deep, the spirit knows.

Convergence of Stars

In velvet skies, stars dance and play,
A cosmic ballet in the Milky Way.
Each twinkle shares a tale of light,
A vivid dream that takes to flight.

Galaxies whisper, secrets unfold,
In hues of silver and hints of gold.
Their paths converge in silent grace,
A canvas vast, a boundless space.

Time stands still, the universe spins,
In every heart, a journey begins.
Constellations guide the lost and found,
In harmony, where dreams abound.

Awake, dear soul, and reach for more,
For in this cosmos, you will soar.
The stars align, and fates entwine,
In cosmic truth, your light will shine.

So breathe in deep, embrace the night,
Let starlit wonders bring you light.
For in the dance of stars above,
Awaits the song of endless love.

Shadows Revealing Light

In dusk's embrace, shadows creep,
A gentle quiet, the world asleep.
Yet in darkness, secrets hide,
Awaiting dawn, when hope shall bide.

Each shadow tells a tale unseen,
Of loss and love, of what has been.
They stretch and twist, yet bring to mind,
The light within, so intertwined.

As sunrise breaks with golden hue,
The whispered dreams begin anew.
From hidden depths, the colors rise,
Transforming dark to brightened skies.

With every layer, truths do share,
The moments lost, the memories rare.
The light reveals what once was veiled,
In shadows deep, the heart resailed.

So cherish night, for at its end,
Is light reborn, a loyal friend.
In every shadow, find your spark,
For in the light, your journey's arc.

Awakening to Truth

In the dawn's gentle glow,
Shadows fade and reveal,
A whisper of clarity,
The heart starts to feel.

Through the veil of the night,
A flicker ignites bold dreams,
The soul yearns for wisdom,
In silence, it gleams.

Eyes open to the light,
Vows once spoken anew,
Courage rises within,
To embrace what is true.

The echoes of laughter,
Dance on the fresh morn,
Configuration of hope,
In each spirit reborn.

With each step in the sun,
The past drifts away,
Awakening to truth,
In the warmth of the day.

The Instant of Revelation

A crack in the stillness,
A spark in the night,
All the pieces converge,
In a moment so bright.

Fingers brush against fate,
Breath quickens with fear,
Time spirals to hold,
What was always right here.

In the hush, understanding,
A world comes alive,
Truth like a river,
In the heart starts to thrive.

Colors pulse and shimmer,
New paths intertwine,
With each breath of insight,
The stars realign.

In the instant of knowing,
The universe sings,
Joy finds its rhythm,
Through delicate wings.

Time Stands Still

In the midst of a storm,
Where chaos entwines,
A pause in the heartbeat,
The balance of lines.

With a glance exchanged softly,
Moments freeze in their grace,
The world takes a breath,
In this transient space.

Thoughts drift like petals,
On a still, quiet lake,
Each ripple, a whisper,
Of dreams we must make.

Feet grounded in wonder,
Eyes locked on the skies,
Here in the stasis,
We watch as time flies.

In the silence of being,
The heart finds its way,
Time stands still for a dream,
In the light of the day.

Unraveled Threads

In the tapestry worn,
Old stories unfold,
Each thread that was tangled,
Now shines pure gold.

With fingers of patience,
We sift through the past,
What was lost yields to hope,
The shadows are cast.

Every knot, every twist,
Tells a tale of its own,
A journey of hearts,
In the fabric we've sewn.

As the loom hums softly,
And colors intertwine,
Unraveled, yet stronger,
Each story divine.

From the chaos of yarns,
A pattern takes flight,
In the dance of our lives,
We find love in the light.

The Revelation within

In silence deep, I strive to see,
The shadows whisper, setting me free.
A heart in turmoil, seeking the light,
Unveiling truths, in the still of night.

Each secret shared, in fervent sighs,
Beneath the veil, no more disguise.
The echoes call from realms unknown,
A journey inward, seeds are sown.

A flicker glows, where hope resides,
In depths of pain, the spirit guides.
Through fractured dreams, a tapestry weaved,
The revelation blooms, once believed.

With gentle hands, I lift the weight,
Embracing love, inviting fate.
With every breath, a shift of view,
In newfound strength, my spirit grew.

In sacred space, I find my voice,
With every choice, I claim my choice.
The past now fades, a distant star,
The revelation, who we are.

A New Horizon Beckons

A whisper stirs, in the morning dew,
Awakening dreams, the skies turn blue.
With every step, I leave behind,
The shadows of doubt, once intertwined.

A canvas wide, the future glows,
In every heartbeat, the promise grows.
Mountains rise, yet I stand tall,
With hope as my guide, I shall not fall.

Winds of change, they sweep the land,
As time unfolds, we take a stand.
With open arms, I greet the dawn,
For in this moment, I'm reborn.

A palette rich, with colors bright,
Painting my path, under soft twilight.
The horizon calls, my spirit soars,
Beyond the limits, I seek the shores.

Adventurous hearts, together we fly,
In unity strong, we touch the sky.
With dreams as fuel, we pave the way,
A new horizon is here to stay.

The Change in the Air

Softly the breeze begins to shift,
As nature whispers, a potent gift.
Branches sway and flowers bloom,
In the heart of spring, dispelling gloom.

Each breath we take is laced with chance,
A dance of fate, in fate's own glance.
The stars align, and worlds collide,
As time unfolds, we cast aside.

A spark ignites, kindling the fire,
Transforming dreams into desire.
With every turn, the cycle spins,
In change we trust, new life begins.

Moments weave, a fragile thread,
In this tapestry, hope is fed.
The change in the air brings forth rebirth,
A shimmering light on this shared earth.

With open hearts, let's boldly sail,
On winds of courage, we shall prevail.
In harmony's song, we find our way,
The change in the air is here to stay.

The Alchemy of Truth

In shadows cast, we find the gold,
Whispers of secrets, softly told.
The heart's elixir, pure and bright,
Turns dreams to lands of radiant light.

In every doubt, a flicker shines,
Threads of fate, the world designs.
With patience, lead begins to gleam,
Transforming loss into a dream.

Through tangled paths, the seekers roam,
Each step a dance toward the unknown.
With open minds, we pave our way,
In every truth, a new display.

The mirror shows, what's deep inside,
Reflections vast as ocean's tide.
Embrace the journey, let it flow,
In alchemy, our spirits grow.

Tumult of Recognition

In crowded rooms, we search for peace,
Faces dance, a wild release.
Familiar strangers, yet unknown,
In their eyes, our paths have grown.

A glance exchanged, the world ignites,
Silent stories, shared insights.
In every laugh, a spark, a thread,
Binding hearts with words unsaid.

As echoes fade, we draw the line,
Life unfolds in twists divine.
With every heartbeat, we collide,
In truth and chaos, we confide.

Reflections mirror, souls seek light,
In shadows cast, we find our sight.
The tumult brews, yet calm appears,
In shared moments, we conquer fears.

The Bridge to New Horizons

Between the worlds, a bridge extends,
Where dreams align, and time transcends.
With courage found in hearts aflame,
We step beyond, make life our game.

Each heartbeat pulses, guiding ways,
Into the dawn of brighter days.
The horizon beckons, bold and near,
With open arms, dispelling fear.

Striding forth on paths untried,
With every choice, we turn the tide.
In unity, hope's whispers soar,
Together strong, we seek much more.

Each step a journey, each breath a chance,
In the flow of time, we boldly dance.
Visions painted on the sky,
A tapestry where dreams can fly.

Serendipity in the Everyday

In morning light, the world awakes,
With whispered hopes that fate remakes.
A simple smile can change the game,
Serendipity, sparking flame.

Amidst the rush of life's embrace,
Moments bloom, pure grace in space.
In every stumble, a hidden gift,
A gentle nudge, the spirit's lift.

The coffee spills, the laughter rings,
In chaos found, the joy it brings.
Through everyday, the magic flows,
In every heart, a story grows.

From chance encounters and random sights,
The universe conspires in flights.
In routine's arms, adventure glows,
Serendipity, the heart bestows.

Signs Written in the Sky

Clouds drift lazily by,
Whispers of dreams unspoken.
Stars flicker in the night,
Messages softly broken.

The moon hums a sweet tune,
Guiding lost souls to shore.
Constellations dance above,
With tales of lovers and war.

Each comet a fleeting thought,
Written in the cosmic ink.
A canvas vast and wide,
Where secrets refuse to sink.

The horizon paints its hue,
In shades of orange and gold.
Sunrise's warm embrace,
A promise gently told.

As day breaks into light,
The signs start to fade away.
Yet in the hearts of dreamers,
The magic will always stay.

A Door Ajar

The door stands slightly open,
Inviting whispers and sighs.
A glimpse of warm yellow light,
Where shadows dance and rise.

Footsteps echo softly near,
With secrets woven tight.
What lies behind that threshold,
In the cocoon of the night?

Curiosity pulls at strings,
A heart races, a breath caught.
What adventures call within,
In the space that time forgot?

Old wood creaks under touch,
Memories linger and play.
Each crack and faded painting,
Holds stories of yesterday.

With an inch of hope and fear,
Will I step beyond the line?
A world of wonder awaits,
If this heart learns to shine.

The World Fell Away

One moment, all was steady,
The ground beneath me shook.
In a swirl of dust and chaos,
I lost my favorite book.

Mountains crumbled like paper,
Rivers wandered astray.
Time itself took a backseat,
As the world fell away.

Voices echoed in silence,
Forgotten dreams in decay.
What once felt so tangible,
In shadows started to sway.

Yet in the heart of the storm,
A flicker of hope burned bright.
As everything drifted apart,
I found my strength to fight.

So when the dust finally settled,
And the sun broke through the gray,
I learned that even in falling,
New wings can find their way.

Notes of a Forgotten Song

There's a melody in the air,
Soft and sweet, just out of reach.
It lingers in the silence,
A lesson it longs to teach.

Once filled with vibrant laughter,
Now echoes in the breeze.
Notes that drift like autumn leaves,
Carried high above the trees.

Each chord holds distant memories,
Of moments lost in time.
A song once sung with fervor,
Now a whisper, faint in rhyme.

I hum it to the starlight,
Searching for what it means.
In the hush of night's embrace,
It rekindles faded dreams.

So let me sing it softly,
With hope in every breath.
For even the forgotten,
Can live on after death.

The Unfolding of Destiny

In the silence of dawn's embrace,
Dreams unfurl like petals in space.
Choices made, paths intertwine,
Each moment a sign, divinely designed.

Whispers of fate, softly weave,
What we believe, we shall receive.
With every step, we tread with grace,
Finding our place in time and space.

Like rivers flow through valleys wide,
We navigate the currents with pride.
The heart knows where it must go,
Guided by a light, a gentle glow.

The canvas of life, colors bright,
We paint our stories with endless light.
Each brushstroke a tale of the soul,
Crafting our journey, making us whole.

In the twilight, destiny calls,
Answering echoes within the walls.
With courage, we unfold the dreams,
Embracing the future as it gleams.

Threads of Fate Unspooling

Tangled threads in the loom of night,
Weaving stories in silver light.
Each strand a life, a tale to tell,
Intertwined in the gentle swell.

Fate dances softly, a wisp in the air,
Spooling moments, tender and rare.
In the tapestry spun by hands unseen,
Lives connect in patterns serene.

The weaver's touch, so deft and kind,
A map of hearts, forever aligned.
Through trials faced and joys embraced,
A fabric of love is interlaced.

Time's gentle fingers, pulling and tugging,
Expose the truths that keep on flooding.
In the grand design, we find our way,
Threads of fate guiding us each day.

As daylight fades and shadows loom,
The future beckons, flowers bloom.
With love as the thread, our fates unite,
In the fabric of life, we shine so bright.

The Constellation of Understanding

In the night sky, stars align,
Illuminating truths, divine.
Each point of light, a thought profound,
In silence, wisdom doth abound.

Galaxies whisper, secrets shared,
In every heart, a soul laid bare.
The cosmos speaks in gentle hues,
Unlocking paths, revealing clues.

Constellations drawn in cosmic ink,
Lead us gently to the brink.
Of knowledge vast, we reach and strive,
In understanding, we truly thrive.

Beneath the universe's vast expanse,
We find connection, a sacred dance.
What once was lost now comes to light,
In the stillness of the night.

Embracing all that we can see,
With open hearts, we seek to be.
In the constellation's warm embrace,
We discover truth, we find our place.

Flickers of Awareness

In the quiet, sparks ignite,
Fleeting moments, pure delight.
A breath, a glance, a fleeting touch,
Awakens worlds, oh so much.

Like fireflies in the dark of night,
Flickers dance, bringing insight.
Awareness blooms in gentle wings,
Revealing the beauty that life brings.

With every heartbeat, echoes grow,
In whispers soft, they gently flow.
The soul awakens, eyes anew,
In vibrant shades, the world feels true.

Through ordinary days, we find,
The magic that resides in mind.
In silence, stillness, we discern,
The simple lessons we must learn.

A gentle nudge, a soft embrace,
In every moment, we find grace.
Flickers of awareness guide our way,
Illuminating the path each day.

An Inner Voice Resounds

In quiet moments, whispers rise,
A gentle echo, truth disguised.
A calling soft, yet clear as day,
It guides the heart along the way.

Amidst the noise, the world can shout,
This inner voice, it won't back out.
It speaks of courage, hope, and grace,
A steady pulse, in life's embrace.

When doubts arise, it holds me tight,
Illuminating paths of light.
Each word a spark, igniting fire,
I follow close, I can't retire.

With every choice, it points the way,
Transforming night into the day.
Bridging gaps 'twixt mind and soul,
An inner voice, it makes me whole.

A symphony that sings within,
A dance of joy where dreams begin.
In silence deep, its strength I'll find,
This inner voice, forever kind.

Captured by the Moment

A fleeting glance, a touch of grace,
Time pauses in this sacred space.
The world around, it fades away,
As hearts connect in bright array.

A whispered laugh, the warmth of light,
Moments shared, a pure delight.
Captured smiles, the stories told,
In every frame, a joy unfolds.

A heartbeat close, the seconds blend,
In every look, a love we send.
These tiny sparks, they light the way,
Turning now into our stay.

Each blink a treasure, each sigh a song,
Until the morning, we drift along.
An essence held, no need to rush,
In stillness found, we find our hush.

Together caught, like dreams entwined,
Each fleeting instant, so defined.
Captured by the moment's grace,
Our hearts will always find their place.

The Bridge to Clarity

Across the chasm, doubts reside,
Yet hope remains, a steadfast guide.
The bridge appears, it beckons me,
To cross the void, to set me free.

With every step, the fog recedes,
New insights grow from hidden seeds.
The path unfolds, revealing light,
Clarity shines, within my sight.

A breath of peace, a gentle sway,
I find my courage, lead the way.
Each question posed ignites the fire,
In search of truth, I won't tire.

The doubts dissolve like morning mist,
With every moment, a new twist.
I cross the bridge, I break the chain,
Embracing clarity, no more pain.

A stronger self, renewed and bold,
In every heartbeat, tales retold.
The bridge to clarity, I embrace,
A journey rich, a sacred space.

Finding the Missing Puzzle Piece

In scattered thoughts and memories,
A quest begins, a gentle breeze.
Each fragment holds a part of me,
Creating whole, a mystery.

I search the nooks, the hidden seams,
Reviving softly faded dreams.
A puzzle piece that fits just right,
Bringing harmony to the night.

With every turn, I chase the clue,
The picture forms, revealing you.
Moments cherished, deep and wide,
The missing piece, no need to hide.

As layers shed, I start to see,
The beauty in my history.
In joyful chaos, patterns rise,
Completing me beneath the skies.

As songs of old weave into now,
Context shines, and I allow.
The missing piece, now found in grace,
A journey woven, time and space.

The Moment I Took Flight

Beneath the vast and open sky,
I felt my spirit start to soar.
Wings unfurled, I learned to fly,
Leaving footprints on the shore.

The wind whispered soft and clear,
Guiding me through clouds above.
In that moment, I conquered fear,
Found my strength, and felt the love.

The world below, a distant dream,
Colors dancing, light aglow.
No longer just a silent scream,
I embraced the chance to grow.

With every beat, my heart took flight,
Carving through the endless blue.
In that moment, pure delight,
A journey vibrant and brand new.

Time suspended, hours blurred,
Holding onto windswept grace.
In my soul, no longer stirred,
I found my home in boundless space.

A Tapestry of Truth

Threads of stories, intertwined,
We weave our past with every thread.
Through laughter, tears, we find our mind,
In colors vibrant, much is said.

Each moment captured, softly spun,
A design that curves and flows.
From struggles faced, to victories won,
In the loom of life, truth grows.

The patterns shift, but still remain,
Anchored deep in who we are.
Through joy and heartache, love and pain,
Our tapestry shines like a star.

In shared embrace, our stories blend,
Creating beauty in the light.
A bond that time cannot suspend,
United, we take flight at night.

With every stitch, each thread we choose,
A reminder of the paths we've crossed.
In this fabric, we shall not lose,
For in truth lies what we've embossed.

A Glimpse Beyond

In twilight's glow, I seek a sign,
A world beyond this earthly stage.
In dreams and whispers, I align,
Unraveling the cosmic page.

Shadows dance with fading light,
Painted hues of life's embrace.
Each heartbeat ends, yet feels so right,
A journey into boundless space.

The stars reveal a hidden path,
Guiding souls through timeless seas.
In their glow, I sense the wrath,
And wisdom of forgotten trees.

Moments fleeting, yet they stay,
Carved in heartbeats, layered deep.
Both night and dawn share the sway,
In silence, dreams awake from sleep.

With every breath, I chase the light,
A glimpse beyond the universe.
Through veils of time, bold and bright,
A longing soul, in wonder, immersed.

Diary of an Awakening

Within the pages, secrets lie,
A whisper to the silent years.
As dawn approaches, shadows die,
Revealing thoughts, the heart now clears.

In tangled webs of hope and doubt,
Each word a step towards the sun.
With every tear, I break out,
A quiet battle fought and won.

The ink flows softly, truths unfold,
Recalling dreams I once let go.
In every line, a story told,
Of courage found and seeds to grow.

Embrace the moments, fleeting fast,
As pages turn, I find my way.
In the present, shadows cast,
But light is born in bright array.

This diary is a journey's start,
An awakening of the soul.
Through written words, I seek my heart,
Finding peace, becoming whole.

The Weight of Knowledge

In dusty tomes, the answers lie,
Bound in leather, reaching for the sky.
Each word a step, each thought a climb,
Defining moments, echoing time.

Heavy hangs the crown of facts,
In silence, intellect contracts.
Yet through the fog, a light appears,
Piercing through the veil of fears.

Pages whisper of battles fought,
In shadows of wisdom, peace is sought.
To know is power; to learn is grace,
Navigating life in a complex space.

With every lesson, burdens grow,
Yet strength is found in what we know.
A paradox within our grasp,
The weight of knowledge, we must clasp.

So ponder deep, explore the vast,
For knowledge gained can hold us fast.
Yet those who share know true delight,
As stories weave through day and night.

Rivers of Revelation

A gentle flow, the river gleams,
Reflecting hopes, and whispered dreams.
Each bend reveals a secret tide,
Where thoughts unearth what hearts confide.

From depths of silence, wisdom springs,
The current carries what truth brings.
Drifting gently, lost in thought,
In every ripple, lessons caught.

Nature's canvas, painted wide,
In flowing waters, mysteries bide.
With every stone, a story flows,
In the quiet depths, the river knows.

A journey long, through bends and turns,
Where every heart grows and learns.
So sail the waters, brave and free,
In rivers deep, find clarity.

Let currents guide you, take the chance,
To dance with fate, to dream and prance.
For in the depths, the soul awakens,
In rivers of revelation, truth is taken.

The Pulse of Discovery

In quiet corners, echoes call,
Awake the seeker, hear the thrall.
A beating heart, alive with quest,
To find the answers, never rest.

Each step ignites a flame anew,
A spark of wonder shining through.
With curious eyes, we roam the night,
In shadows dance, in search of light.

Questions arise like stars that gleam,
Pulling us deeper into the dream.
The pulse of discovery calls us near,
Through paths unknown, we shed our fear.

Unraveling threads of time and space,
Finding our place, embracing grace.
Each revelation, a story spun,
In the dance of life, we are all one.

So chase the whispers, heed the sighs,
For in the unknown, our spirit flies.
With passion bold and hearts aflame,
The pulse of discovery fuels our name.

A Spark Among the Shadows

In corners dark, where doubts reside,
A flicker glows, a light inside.
Against the night, it starts to rise,
A spark igniting hopeful skies.

With every breath, the flame expands,
A beacon born from trembling hands.
Through fears it flickers, fiercely bright,
To push away the heavy night.

In shadows deep, creation breathes,
With whispered truths, the heart believes.
A spark of courage, bold and true,
To light the path for me and you.

So do not fear the dark's embrace,
For every shadow hides a grace.
In the quiet, hear the call,
A spark among the shadows, we find all.

Embrace the glow, let spirits soar,
In light we find what hearts adore.
Together strong, hand in hand,
With sparks of hope, we take a stand.

The Harvest of Understanding

In fields of wisdom, we sow our seeds,
Nurtured by questions, fulfilling our needs.
The sun of insight shines bright overhead,
Guiding our journey, where knowledge is spread.

Each grain of thought, a treasure to find,
Gathers like whispers, the heart and the mind.
Together they grow, intertwined and strong,
In the harvest of truth, we all belong.

As seasons pass by, the fruits come alive,
A banquet of knowledge where we all thrive.
We feast on the lessons that life has to share,
In the harvest of understanding, we care.

With open arms, we embrace the new light,
Finding our way through the shadows of night.
Each echo of reason, a bridge to cross,
In the garden of thought, we gain what was lost.

Together we stand, we cherish the gains,
Reflecting on struggles, the losses, the pains.
With hearts full of love, we gather once more,
In the harvest of understanding, we soar.

Labyrinths of Thought and Clarity

In maze-like twists, our minds often roam,
Seeking the pathways that lead us back home.
With each turn we take, confusion may reign,
Yet clarity shines through the fog and the rain.

As shadows dance round, whispers call from afar,
Navigating corners, we follow a star.
While echoes of doubt may cloud what we see,
The heart holds the compass, guiding us free.

With pencil and paper, we sketch out the lines,
Mapping our journey through dares and designs.
In the labyrinth deep, every step shows the way,
To clarity's light, where we long to stay.

Through thickets of doubt, we patiently tread,
Piecing together the truths that we've read.
With courage and thought, we break from the bind,
Emerging victorious, our purpose defined.

So when paths get tangled, remember to breathe,
Amidst the confusion, your soul will believe.
For in the labyrinths, both chaos and grace,
Is the essence of thought, where clarity waits.

Embracing the Inherent Truth

In silence we seek the truth that resides,
Within every heart, where authenticity hides.
With open arms, we summon our fears,
Embracing the lessons learned through our tears.

The mirror reflects both the light and the shade,
In honesty's gaze, we refuse to evade.
For the truth that we gather, the stories we weave,
Are threads of connection in what we believe.

With each revelation, a spark comes alive,
Illuminating pathways on which we must strive.
United in purpose, we journey as one,
In the embrace of truth, our fears come undone.

Together we stand on this fragile ground,
In the richness of honesty, love is profound.
We cherish the moments, the struggles we've faced,
For in truth, we find strength, our spirits embraced.

So let us walk forward with courage and grace,
Embracing our stories, our journeys we trace.
In the heart of our fabric, we find what is true,
As we gather together, me and you.

The Fabric of Uncertainty

In threads of chaos, we stitch and we weave,
The tapestry of life, difficult to perceive.
What lies ahead is a mystery still,
Yet in moments of doubt, we learn to be still.

Each knot that we tie holds a lesson within,
Of courage and hope, where our journeys begin.
In the fabric of life, every tear and fray,
Tells stories of strength, shaping who we are today.

With hearts open wide, we embrace what may come,
Navigating futures that make us feel numb.
Yet through the uncertainty, we find our own way,
Creating a masterpiece with each passing day.

So dance with the shadows, sing with the light,
In the fabric we craft, let the heart take flight.
For woven together, with love in each seam,
Is the beauty of life and the power of dream.

The threads bind us closer in the ebb and flow,
In uncertainty's arms, let your spirit grow.
With every experience, new patterns arise,
In the fabric of life, our potential lies.

An Opening to New Realities

In the hush of dawn's embrace,
New paths call in whispered grace.
Eyes wide to the world's vast play,
Every moment a new ballet.

Veils lift softly from the mind,
Wonders waiting to be kind.
Changes dance in vibrant hues,
Each heartbeat brings the chance to choose.

Stepping forth with courage bright,
Navigating through the light.
Possibilities stretch and soar,
The future opens, evermore.

Beneath the stars, dreams align,
Infinite threads of fate entwine.
Unlock the door; let visions flow,
Beyond the known, the spirits glow.

In this space of boundless might,
Awakened souls ignite the night.
Together we shall chart the skies,
Where every fear and doubt denies.

The Awakening of Dreams

In the cradle of night's still hold,
A tapestry of dreams unfolds.
Whispers linger on the breeze,
Where hopes arise with gentle ease.

Each star a story yet to tell,
In the quiet where shadows dwell.
Hearts ignited, spirits bold,
Chasing visions of pure gold.

Awakening with dawn's bright kiss,
Moments blended into bliss.
With every breath, the past released,
Embracing now, our souls increased.

Gathering strength from wisdom's fire,
Fueling the heart's deep desire.
As horizons shift and bend,
We find unity, all extend.

Together weaving dreamer's grace,
In every heart, a sacred space.
Awake to life, in vibrant streams,
In the journey, live the dreams.

A Kaleidoscope of Insight

Life's prism bends with every glance,
Colors shift in a fleeting dance.
Thoughts collide, then intertwine,
A landscape rich, a grand design.

Perception blooms in myriad forms,
Within the stillness, the chaos warms.
Fractals spin, revealing now,
The truth through which we humbly bow.

Moments sharpen, wisdom grows,
In tangled paths, clarity flows.
Every twist opens new views,
An endless canvas of life's hues.

In silence, find what's softly said,
A symphony of hearts & heads.
Listen deeply, seek the core,
Within the kaleidoscope, explore.

Through this lens, the world aligns,
With endless tales and ancient signs.
Holding light through each new phase,
A tapestry of insight stays.

Living in the Light of Knowing

Awareness blooms in radiant dawn,
In each heartbeat, we are drawn.
To illuminate what lies ahead,
In every thought, our truths are spread.

Clarity dances, shadows sway,
Revealing paths we've lost along the way.
With open hearts and minds so free,
We step into our destiny.

Wisdom whispers in the breeze,
Unveiling secrets with such ease.
Every choice, a spark of flame,
In this light, we rise, reclaim.

Living bright, our spirits rise,
In every moment, the magic lies.
To know, to feel, to simply be,
In the light of knowing, we see me.

Together, bound by endless ties,
In shared knowing, the spirit flies.
Here in unity, we find our sight,
Living fully in the light.

Recognition in the Silence

In the stillness, whispers fade,
Echoes of thoughts are gently laid.
A heartbeats' rhythm, soft and clear,
In silence, truths begin to steer.

Through the quiet, meaning flows,
Amidst the calm, a spirit glows.
In every pause, a chance to see,
The beauty found in glimmering glee.

Voices unheard, yet always near,
In the silence, we hold dear.
A canvas blank, yet vividly bright,
Where recognition takes its flight.

Whispers linger, softly bind,
To the secrets we might find.
As shadows shift and fade away,
In silence, we begin to sway.

Moments cherished, softly caught,
In the stillness, all is thought.
With every breath, we gently kneel,
And find the truths we long to feel.

The Horizon Brightens

At dawn's embrace, the world awakes,
With hues of gold, the darkness breaks.
The sun ascends, a fiery glow,
Across the sky, the warmth will flow.

Clouds drift slowly, like dreams on air,
Each moment laced with gentle flair.
Upon the waves, reflections dance,
A glimmering touch, life's sweet chance.

Hope unfurls with every ray,
In silent whispers, the night must stay.
A promise blooms with morning's light,
The horizon brightens, future in sight.

Birds take flight, a joyful sound,
As nature sings, with love unbound.
Each heartbeat syncs with dawn's new song,
Together, we find where we belong.

The warmth of day, a sweet embrace,
Guiding our steps, a steady pace.
As shadows fade and dreams take form,
The horizon brightens, a new norm.

Shadows of Doubt Dispelled

In the corners where fears reside,
Shadows linger, but cannot hide.
With patience and light, they fade away,
Leaving hope for a brighter day.

Whispers of doubt, they may arise,
Yet courage grows as we realize.
With every step, the fog recedes,
A strength awakened, fulfilling needs.

Voices of past may try to sway,
But we stand firm, come what may.
With every breath, we choose to rise,
Shadows dispelled as love implies.

Lessons learned from struggles faced,
In the light, we find our place.
The past, a guide, yet not a chain,
In the journey, we grow from pain.

Illuminate the paths we tread,
No longer bound by what we dread.
With hope as our lantern, we shall tell,
The story of shadows that once befell.

The Spark of Insight

In silence waits a flickering spark,
A thought ignites within the dark.
With clarity born from stillness found,
Wisdom whispers, profound and sound.

Moments pause, and minds take flight,
Illuminated by newfound light.
Ideas flourish, a gentle breeze,
Thoughts interweave with joyous ease.

Each question posed reveals a thread,
Leading to paths where dreams are fed.
Discoveries bloom like flowers bright,
In the garden of the mind's insight.

With gentle strokes, new visions paint,
The canvas vast, the heart a saint.
Through trials faced and lessons learned,
The spark of insight, brightly burned.

Embrace the muse, let thoughts entwine,
In every moment, our stars align.
Infinite journeys await, unfold,
With each spark, new stories told.

The Elysian Moment

In the hush of twilight's grace,
Whispers weave through time's embrace.
Stars awaken, dreams take flight,
Hearts unite in soft delight.

Laughter spins on gentle breeze,
As nature hums its tender keys.
Colors blend in passion's dance,
In this moment, life's romance.

Echoes of a past unknown,
In stillness, seeds of hope are sown.
Each heartbeat sings a sacred hymn,
In the light where shadows swim.

Time dissolves in sacred glow,
In the quiet, spirits flow.
Every sigh a promise made,
In the twilight's gentle shade.

Here we stand, no need to roam,
Finding peace in moments' dome.
Elysium wrapped in a sigh,
With love's wings, we learn to fly.

Harbinger of Change

The winds howl with tales untold,
A shift in fate, both fierce and bold.
Old leaves fall, a new dawn breaks,
Time to rise, for life awakes.

In shadows cast by fleeting light,
Hope emerges, burning bright.
Voices lift, the silence shatters,
As every dream, through chaos, scatters.

Chains of doubt begin to rust,
Carried forth by faith and trust.
Rivers flow with courage's might,
Steering hearts through darkest night.

With each heartbeat, futures bloom,
From corners dark, we shred the gloom.
Change ignites the world anew,
In the depths, life finds its cue.

Embrace the storm, ride the tide,
In every whisper, hope will guide.
For every end births something grand,
A harvest rich from barren land.

The Map to Inner Landscapes

A compass spun within the heart,
Guides us through the shadows' art.
Paths untaken, dreams unfold,
In silence, stories will be told.

Mountains rise, valleys dip low,
In each moment, seeds we sow.
Reflections dance on waters clear,
Echoes of all we hold dear.

Whispers beckon from the deep,
Ancient truths gently leap.
Journey inward, seek the light,
As stars emerge from endless night.

Each step taken, courage gained,
Through tangled woods, love is claimed.
With open hearts, we walk this land,
Finding strength in where we stand.

Maps are drawn in tender grace,
With every breath, we find our place.
Inner worlds, vast and wide,
Guide us where our hopes reside.

Breakthrough Beneath the Layers

In layers thick, the truth does hide,
Yet underneath, the heart's a guide.
With open eyes, we peel away,
To find the light of breaking day.

Tangled roots in fertile ground,
Awakening where hope is found.
Voices rise from depths of pain,
For every loss, there's much to gain.

The storms may rage, the winds will howl,
Yet through it all, we learn to growl.
Resilience blooms in cracks of stone,
With unity, we build our throne.

As shadows fall, we find our way,
Together, we can seize the day.
From hidden dreams, we break the mold,
With every heartbeat, brave and bold.

Through broken wings, the soul will soar,
For underneath, we are much more.
In layers deep, our truth shall sing,
Of love, of life, of awakening.

Beyond the Fog of Confusion

In shadows thick, where thoughts collide,
A maze of doubts, where fears abide.
Yet through the mist, a whisper calls,
To guide the heart where reason falls.

With every step, the path grows clear,
The fog dissolves, and dreams draw near.
A dawning light, a gentle hand,
Leading us forth to understand.

Through tangled minds and restless nights,
We search for truth, we seek the lights.
Beyond the fog, our vision lowered,
A world reborn, a soul empowered.

Embrace the quest, the journey wide,
For in confusion, strength will bide.
Each twist and turn, a lesson learned,\nIn foggy realms, our hearts have yearned.

With clearer eyes, we start anew,
An open heart, a sky of blue.
Beyond the haze, our spirits soar,
Together we rise, forevermore.

Dancing with Certainty.

In the glow of the moonlit night,
We twirl and spin, our souls in flight.
With every step, we claim our space,
In this ballet of time and grace.

The rhythm beats within our chests,
A pulse of truth that never rests.
With every turn, our doubts retreat,
As certainty guides our moving feet.

The world fades dim, but we ignite,
A spark of joy, a burst of light.
In the dance of life, we find our way,
Embracing now, come what may.

Our feet gliding on the floor of dreams,
Boundless hope in radiant beams.
With certainty as our trusted friend,
We dance with fervor, until the end.

Through every stumble, we rise anew,
In unison, together we flew.
With each heartbeat, under stars so bright,
We find our truth in the endless night.

The Moment Clarity Arrived

In silence deep, the noise subsides,
A gentle whisper, where it abides.
And then, a spark ignites the dark,
The dawn of thought, a guiding mark.

Like a river flowing, smooth and deep,
The truth takes shape, in heart we keep.
Beyond the clouds, the sun will shine,
Revealing paths that intertwine.

A word, a glance, a sudden chance,
From chaos born, a cosmic dance.
In fragmented dreams, we see the whole,
The moment clarity claims the soul.

With every breath, the fog dissolves,
Our questions fade as the truth evolves.
In that instant, light prevails,
We find the strength in gentle tales.

Mind unfurling, like petals wide,
In the garden of thought, we now reside.
For clarity brings a peace so rare,
A sweet embrace, a love laid bare.

Unveiling the Hidden Truth

Beneath the layers, secrets sleep,
In silent depths, where shadows creep.
With patient hands, we peel away,
The veils of doubt that mock the day.

In hidden corners, whispers swell,
A tale untold, a magic spell.
As light breaks through, we start to see,
The heartbeat of what's meant to be.

With every step, the truth revealed,\nA tapestry of dreams unsealed.
In sacred spaces, wisdom weaves,
A vibrant thread that never leaves.

Through trials faced and battles fought,
In every scar, a lesson taught.
The hidden truth, we claim with grace,
Embracing journeys we now embrace.

With open hearts, we choose to seek,
In every silence, every peak.
For within us lies the greatest part,
The unveiled truth that stirs the heart.

The Gentle Nudge of Insight

In silence whispers truth at night,
A flicker guides the wandering sight.
With gentle hands, it shapes the heart,
Embracing realms where thoughts depart.

The mind awakes to deeper tones,
In quietude, the wisdom sown.
Each moment holds a sacred spark,
Illuminating paths through dark.

A subtle shift, a breath anew,
Reveals the world in vibrant hue.
Connections bridge the void of fear,
And love expands, forever near.

The gentle nudge, a sweet caress,
In every pause, we learn to bless.
Through layers peeled, our essence shines,
A tapestry of grand designs.

So let the whispers guide your way,
In stillness find the songs we play.
With gratitude, embrace the light,
Awakened souls take joyous flight.

Chasing the Glow of Knowing

With every step, the journey starts,
A lantern flickers in our hearts.
A flicker leads to grasping hands,
Chasing the glow that understanding grants.

In shadows cast by doubt and fear,
Resilience blooms when truth is near.
Through every trial, we seek to find,
The essence of a curious mind.

Mountains stood and valleys wide,
In search of wisdom, we confide.
The path may twist, but hope won't cease,
In every question, there's a peace.

The stars above, a guide to see,
Each glow reflects our unity.
With every heartbeat, echoes flow,
The thrill of chasing what we know.

So onward we press, through night and day,
With every doubt, we'll find a way.
For in the chase, our spirits grow,
In timeless dance, we find our glow.

The Symphony of Discovery

A melody in whispered breeze,
Invites us to embrace with ease.
In every note, a story weaves,
Through heartstrings pulled, the spirit believes.

The world unfolds, a grand display,
A symphony of night and day.
In rhythms soft, adventures call,
We rise and fall, we stand, we sprawl.

With eyes attuned, we start to see,
Harmony in life's cacophony.
Each moment's beat, a pulse of truth,
Resonating through the years of youth.

In every discord, wisdom's gain,
A chance to learn, to feel the pain.
Together voices soar and blend,
In unity, our hearts will mend.

So let the music lead us on,
In every dusk, in every dawn.
The symphony of life's embrace,
In every note, we find our place.

The Seedling of Awareness

From tiny roots, the journey starts,
Nurtured deep within our hearts.
In gentle soil, the dreams take flight,
A seedling blooms with morning light.

Awareness grows in tender care,
A whisper soft, a breath of air.
The world unfurls, and we convene,
In every moment, calm and keen.

With open eyes, we seek to see,
The beauty in simplicity.
In every touch, in every breath,
The cycle of our lives, in depth.

Nourished by love, we learn to stand,
In unity, a guiding hand.
Through storms that come, we bend, we sway,
With roots that anchor, come what may.

So cherish each small, wondrous seed,
In every challenge, plant the need.
For in awareness, we shall thrive,
A garden rich, where dreams arrive.

Moment of Clarity

In silence deep, the truth revealed,
A heart once blind, now gently healed.
The world in hues, more bright than gray,
A spark ignites, it lights the way.

Thoughts once tangled, now align,
Each breath a gift, each heartbeat, fine.
The past dissolves, a distant ghost,
Embracing now, a joyful host.

In every tear, a lesson learned,
A flicker of hope, a passion burned.
With every step, the path unfolds,
A story fresh, a life retold.

The sky above, a canvas wide,
In every heart, truths do reside.
No longer lost, the fog has cleared,
In every moment, love is steered.

With open arms, I face the light,
A moment of peace, pure and bright.
The past is done, the future waits,
In this clarity, joy radiates.

The Day Everything Changed

A whisper soft, the dawn broke clear,
A heart once bound, now beat sincere.
The clock struck one, a shifting tide,
In shadows deep, new dreams reside.

With every hope, a new path formed,
Through trials faced, my spirit warmed.
I stood alone, yet felt so brave,
A life renewed, no longer a slave.

The clouds that hung, began to shift,
In every challenge, I found a gift.
The world transformed with every glance,
In fate's embrace, I learned to dance.

With open arms to all that's new,
In colors bright, the vision grew.
No more the past, just what can be,
The day of change, alive and free.

With strength restored, I walk ahead,
On paths of gold, where dreams are fed.
The day I chose to break the mold,
A story rich, waiting to be told.

Epiphany at Dawn

As light arrives, the shadows flee,
A sudden truth, just meant for me.
In stillness deep, the world awakes,
A gentle breeze, a heart that shakes.

The universe speaks, through whispers mild,
In every laugh, the joy of a child.
With open eyes, I see it clear,
In every heartbeat, love draws near.

In veils of doubt, the sun breaks through,
With every moment, a chance anew.
The past is gone, like mist in air,
In this fresh dawn, I'm free from care.

With gratitude, each breath I take,
A sacred vow, the world I'll wake.
In harmony, my spirit sings,
At dawn's first light, I spread my wings.

A revelation, pure and bright,
Transforming darkness into light.
With love and grace, I walk this way,
An epiphany, come what may.

A Shift in the Breeze

A gentle wind whispers a change,
Through the trees, it feels so strange.
Leaves dance lightly, a joyful tune,
As sunlight kisses the afternoon.

In every shift, a story told,
Of paths once crossed, of hearts so bold.
The air is thick with dreams and light,
In this new breeze, all feels right.

I close my eyes, and feel it near,
A soft embrace, a breath of cheer.
With every gust, old fears are shed,
In this sweet change, I'm gently led.

Through open fields, I find my way,
In nature's arms, I long to stay.
The world alive, alive with sound,
In the shift of breeze, freedom found.

Each moment flows, like rivers run,
A tapestry woven under the sun.
No longer bound, my spirit free,
In the shift of the breeze, I simply be.

The Dance of Recognizing Self

In shadows deep, I find my spark,
A mirror gleams, revealing the dark.
Steps I take, with grace and care,
Awakening light, so pure and rare.

Whispers of truth begin to chime,
Each heartbeat echoes, marking time.
In the silence, I hear my soul,
A journey inward, to become whole.

Embracing flaws, I learn to rise,
Colors of life, in every guise.
With every twirl, a chance to see,
The dance of recognizing me.

In twilight's glow, I move in peace,
Layers of doubt slowly release.
With every step, I peel away,
The masks I wore, no longer stay.

In this ballet, I feel alive,
In the rhythms, I learn to thrive.
This dance of self, a sacred trance,
Embracing all, my soul's true chance.

Threads of Illumination

In the tapestry of night, stars align,
Each thread of light, a tale divine.
Woven whispers through the cosmic sea,
Unraveling truths that set us free.

Golden fibers of hope and dreams,
Forming patterns, or so it seems.
With every stitch, connections grow,
Threads of illumination start to glow.

In shadows cast, the stories hide,
Seeking the light, where souls abide.
Weaving wisdom in every line,
Guided by fate, so pure, so fine.

With careful touch, I bind the seams,
Crafting visions from silent dreams.
In this design, we find our worth,
Threads of love that cradle the earth.

Through life's fabric, we intertwine,
Each thread a journey, uniquely mine.
Together we shine, a radiant beam,
In the loom of time, we weave our dream.

The Ripple of Insight

A pebble dropped in water's grace,
Creates ripples in a sacred space.
With each wave, a thought unfolds,
Revealing secrets life holds.

Concentric circles spread away,
Echoes of wisdom come to play.
In moments still, clarity blooms,
Shining light in shadowy rooms.

Glimmers of truth dance on the tide,
In each reflection, we confide.
The depths of knowing call my name,
In the current, I find my flame.

With every whisper, insights grow,
A tapestry of knowing flow.
As ripples merge, I understand,
The power of thoughts, as they expand.

So cast your stone, let it gleam,
In the waters of the mind, we dream.
In awareness, we find our way,
The ripple of insight leads the day.

Journey into the Unexpected

A path unfolds, where shadows play,
The unknown calls, I must obey.
With every step, I leave behind,
The map of comfort, now unlined.

Curious winds tousle my hair,
Whispers of wildness fill the air.
In this venture, fears may rise,
Yet courage blooms 'neath open skies.

Encounters strange, yet deeply known,
In foreign lands, seeds are sown.
With open heart, I wander free,
Finding treasures, uniquely me.

The journey twists, like rivers flow,
Through valleys dark, to peaks that glow.
With every turn, new sights unfold,
A tapestry of stories told.

So here I roam, with spirit wide,
Embracing wonders on this ride.
In the unexpected, joy ignites,
My heart, a compass, in endless flights.

Heartbeats of Discovery

In silence, secrets start to bloom,
With every step, we chase the room.
The echoes dance, the shadows play,
New paths unfold, come what may.

Bright stars align, a guiding force,
Each heartbeat leads us, we stay the course.
Through valleys deep, and mountains high,
We forge ahead, beneath the sky.

The whispers call, in the night so clear,
With every glance, we shed our fear.
A journey formed in dreams amassed,
Through unseen doors, we travel fast.

Each turn we take, a lesson learned,
In every corner, passion burned.
With open hearts, we strive and seek,
In every moment, it's truth we speak.

Our spirits rise, like dawn's first light,
With every heartbeat, we ignite.
Together bound, through thick and thin,
In discovery's arms, we begin again.

Awakening from the Dream

In twilight's haze, we start to see,
The lines of life, painted vividly.
Voices linger, soft and low,
Awakening whispers, beckon us to grow.

From slumber's grasp, we break away,
In morning's light, the shadows sway.
The world outside, so bright and bold,
A tapestry of tales unfolds.

With every breath, a chance to feel,
The pulse of love, the moments real.
Each step we take, on firmest ground,
In waking dreams, our truth is found.

Eyes now wide, with wonder bright,
We dance together, hearts take flight.
The beauty found in everyday,
Awakens joy in a wondrous way.

Through valleys deep, and skies so vast,
We cherish now, the love amassed.
With every heartbeat, more we glean,
In the symphony of life, we dream.

Fragments of Realization

In shards of light, we start to see,
The truth that lies inside of me.
Each moment holds a key to share,
Fragments glimmer, beyond compare.

Through tangled woods, we navigate,
In silence, we begin to relate.
Our stories blend, like colors bright,
In every shadow, there shines a light.

With hearts laid bare, we question why,
In every tear, a chance to fly.
The pieces form, a puzzle clear,
In unity, we conquer fear.

In every laugh, in every sigh,
The fragments dance, as we comply.
To learn from pain, to rise anew,
With every heartbeat, we pursue.

The search for truth, it shapes our fate,
In every moment, love's the gate.
With open eyes, we find our way,
In fragments bright, we choose to stay.

The Unveiling

Behind the veil, the truth awaits,
In shadows deep, we find our fates.
With courage bold, we lift the shroud,
In whispered winds, we speak aloud.

The hidden path, a gentle curve,
In every heart, we find the nerve.
With every question, light is cast,
In moments cherished, futures vast.

Revealing layers, one by one,
In every dawn, the journey's fun.
The light cascades, a healing touch,
In the unveiling, we flourish much.

With every glance, there's more to see,
In truth's embrace, we learn to be.
With open hearts, the world expands,
In unity, we take our stands.

The magic lies in being free,
In every heartbeat, harmony.
With each layer shed, we start anew,
In the unveiling, love shines through.

The Path to Unveiling Mysteries

In shadows deep where secrets dwell,
A road unfolds, a tale to tell.
With every step, the mind ignites,
As whispers guide through silent nights.

The moon above, a watchful eye,
Illuminates the dreams that fly.
In quiet corners echo truths,
Where wisdom breathes within our youth.

The stars align, a cosmic sign,
Inviting souls to seek, to shine.
Each turn reveals a hidden door,
Unlocking paths we can't ignore.

Let courage lead, let vision soar,
Embrace the quest, discover more.
The heart's desire, a gentle flame,
Drives us onward, ever the same.

Through tangled vines and endless space,
We find our footing, quicken pace.
In love and light, we set our sail,
On the eternal, winding trail.

Glimpses Beyond the Veil

A shimmer lies at twilight's door,
Invisible threads we can't ignore.
Glimmers of truth pierce the night,
As shadows dance, revealing light.

In silken dreams, the veil is thin,
Whispers beckon from within.
With every heartbeat, visions flow,
In this sacred space, we grow.

Past the illusions, love appears,
Washing away the veils of fears.
Each breath unfolds a new embrace,
Where spirits meet in timeless grace.

The stars above, a guiding spark,
Illuminate the hidden arc.
In fleeting moments, truth we find,
Connecting hearts, uniting minds.

Beyond the veil, hope lingers near,
A tapestry woven from our tears.
Awakened souls, a unified tale,
In the depths, we shall prevail.

The Heart's True Compass

In the quiet stillness of the dawn,
The heart whispers, a gentle song.
It points the way through troubled seas,
Where love resides and sets us free.

With every beat, a pulse of fate,
A guiding force to navigate.
Trust in the rhythm, let it lead,
Through every plant and every seed.

In moments lost, when paths divide,
The heart's true compass will abide.
With courage bold, we face the storm,
For in its warmth, we find our form.

Hopes take flight on wings of dreams,
As life flows on in radiant streams.
The heart, a beacon shining bright,
Illuminates the darkest night.

Through valleys deep and mountains high,
The compass points towards the sky.
In every heart, the truth prevails,
A journey marked by love's own trails.

Unraveling the Threads of Fate

In the tapestry of time we weave,
The threads of fate, a tale to believe.
With every twist, a story unfolds,
Of secrets kept and dreams retold.

The loom of life, with colors bright,
Crafts our journeys through day and night.
With grace, we pull, we gently sway,
As the fabric guides us on our way.

Through tangled paths, we search for signs,
In whispered winds and ancient shrines.
The heart can sense what eyes can't see,
Unraveling all that's meant to be.

With threads of joy and strings of pain,
We sew together what remains.
Each knot a lesson, each tear a flood,
In the great design, we find our blood.

So let us tread with open minds,
And seek the beauty life unwinds.
In every thread, a purpose waits,
Unraveling the intricate fates.

Lifting the Veil

In shadows deep, a whisper stirs,
Secrets hidden, the heart concurs.
A gentle breeze, the night exhales,
Revealing truths as silence pales.

With every breath, the world aligns,
Mysteries dance in moonlit signs.
An unseen hand draws back the shroud,
Insight blooms, both fierce and proud.

Through the darkness, a flicker gleams,
Awakening hopes, igniting dreams.
In quiet moments, wisdom flows,
Lifting the veil where magic grows.

The past and present intertwine,
In whispered tales, the stars combine.
With every heartbeat, life reveals,
A sun-kissed dawn as shadows peel.

Let echoes guide you, past the night,
To realms where visions spark the light.
In unity, our spirits sail,
Together we rise, lifting the veil.

Time's Gentle Nudge

The clock ticks soft, a steady guide,
Moments fleeting, like the tide.
In every breath, a story spins,
Time's gentle nudge, where life begins.

Each second passes, never strays,
Like sunlight fading at end of days.
But memories weave a tapestry,
Rich with laughter, sweet reverie.

In quiet corners, stillness breathes,
Moments cherished, like autumn leaves.
Time whispers softly, yet it sings,
Of love and loss, of endless things.

Embrace the now, the fleeting grace,
Find joy in every small embrace.
Let moments linger, hold them tight,
Time's gentle nudge, a guiding light.

For in this dance of years and days,
We find our path in myriad ways.
Embrace the flow, let spirit rise,
In time's embrace, our hearts are wise.

The Echo Before the Storm

A hush descends, the world holds breath,
In the stillness, a shadowed heft.
The sky is hushed, a trembling pause,
Nature whispers, a silent cause.

Clouds gather round, like thoughts in flight,
An echo stirs, igniting night.
With every heartbeat, tension grows,
The storm approaches, and nature knows.

Lightning flickers, like a spark of fate,
Thunder rumbles, a siren's date.
In that moment, all hearts resonate,
The echo builds, as time will wait.

Then comes the rain, a cleansing sweep,
Awakening echoes from deep sleep.
Chaos dances with wild delight,
The tempest sings, embracing night.

Before the storm, the world prepares,
In the quiet, beauty flares.
With every echo, embrace the norm,
For life ignites in the eye of the storm.

Fragrant Air of Change

The flowers bloom, their colors bright,
In fragrant air, they dance in light.
A whisper flows through branches wide,
In every petal, new hopes abide.

The earth awakens, a vibrant song,
As seasons shift, where we belong.
With gentle hands, the breezes play,
Carrying dreams, inviting sway.

Transformation blooms in every heart,
In fragrant air, we find our part.
Let go of shadows, embrace the sun,
For change is here, and life's begun.

Through winding paths, our spirits soar,
In every challenge, we open doors.
Together we rise, hand in hand,
In fragrant air, a hopeful land.

So breathe in deep, let worries fade,
Embrace the change, be unafraid.
For life's a journey, a precious chance,
In fragrant air, we dare to dance.

The Day Insight Bloomed

In the garden of thoughts, seeds take flight,
Colors of clarity, morning so bright.
With whispers of wisdom, the dawn unfolds,
New paths of intention, a story retold.

Each petal of truth, a lesson to learn,
The heart feels the spark, the mind starts to yearn.
Branches of knowledge stretch wide to the sky,
Fruits of the spirit, in abundance they lie.

No longer confined, the soul breaks its chains,
Dancing in sunlight, as folly wanes.
In the breeze, revelations begin to bloom,
In the light of awareness, shadows find room.

With each grateful breath, I invite the new day,
Embrace the unfolding, let worries drift away.
A promise of growth, with a soft, gentle grace,
The day insight bloomed, all fears now erased.

A Spark in the Shadows

In the corners where silence weaves tales deep,
A flicker of vision wakes dreams from sleep.
Whispers of hope on the edge of despair,
A spark flickers softly, igniting the air.

Hidden behind all the doubts and the fears,
Light dances in shadows, dissolving the tears.
Echoes of courage, a new dawn's refrain,
The heart, once so burdened, begins to unchain.

From ashes of doubt, a fire ignites,
The warmth of acceptance on cold, lonely nights.
Illuminating paths where the lost can roam,
A spark in the shadows beckons us home.

With flickers of insight, our visions collide,
In the quietest corners, we no longer hide.
The glow of connection, so precious, so rare,
A spark in the shadows, igniting the air.

The Whisper of Realization

In stillness, I hear it, a secret so clear,
The whisper of truth, ever drawing me near.
It beckons with warmth, like the sun on my face,
Revealing the beauty in time's gentle pace.

Thoughts dance like leaves in the soft autumn breeze,
As realizations settle with calm, gentle ease.
Each moment a thread, weaving patterns divine,
In the tapestry of life, all things intertwine.

With a heartbeat of silence, the world fades away,
And wisdom arises in its soft ballet.
The whisper of change calls, a promise of light,
In the art of acceptance, releasing the night.

Step into the dawn, where shadows now cease,
Embrace every journey and find your release.
The whisper of realization, a sweet, gentle tone,
In the heart's quiet chamber, we are never alone.

Epiphany in the Midnight Hour

In the stillness of night, when the world dims its glow,
Epiphanies dance in the soft undertow.
Mirrors of silence reflect hidden truths,
As stars spill their secrets upon weary youths.

With a sigh, I release all the burdens I bear,
Embracing the shadows, I find solace there.
The clock ticks in whispers, time gently refrains,
Each moment a treasure where wisdom remains.

As moonlight reveals all that slumbers within,
The dawn of awareness begins to begin.
With clarity gained, like a song without end,
Epiphany whispers, a long-lost friend.

As the veil slowly lifts, old fears fall away,
In the midnight hour, I welcome the day.
Boundless horizons invite me to soar,
Epiphany lingers, forever my core.

A Door Opened by Awareness

A gentle breeze begins to sway,
Whispers of change in the fray.
Eyes once closed begin to see,
A world alive, wild, and free.

The light creeps in, softly it glows,
Casting shadows, revealing what knows.
Thoughts unhurried, drifting like leaves,
Opening doors, the heart believes.

Moments shimmer in the dawn's embrace,
Life unfolds at an effortless pace.
Awareness beckons, urging to feel,
The truth beneath, raw and real.

Each step forward, each breath deep,
Secrets awakened from the sleep.
Courage found in the quiet of night,
Hope ignites, guiding the sight.

Feel the pulse of the universe near,
Echoes of wisdom, crystal clear.
A door opened, inviting the soul,
To dance in the light, to become whole.

The Unmasking of Reality

Behind the curtain, shadows play,
Masks of illusion holding sway.
With each revelation, layers peel,
Truth emerges, raw and real.

The echoes of laughter, the silence of tears,
Unveiling dreams, confronting fears.
The heart beats louder, the spirit sings,
In the unmasking, we find our wings.

Voices intertwined in the cosmic dance,
Each moment offers a second chance.
In the stillness, wisdom flows,
Awakening hearts as the light glows.

Mirrors reflect what we often hide,
In their depths, the truths abide.
As the fog lifts, clarity reigns,
The unmasking of what remains.

Embrace the rawness, cherish the real,
Discover the layers that time reveals.
Together we stand, unafraid to see,
In the unmasking, we are set free.

Reflections of Clarity

In water's stillness, truth appears,
Rippling softly, dissolving fears.
Each reflection tells a tale,
Of journeys taken, where hearts sail.

Through the fog of doubt, visions clear,
Insights emerge when we draw near.
The light within begins to glow,
Guiding us where we need to flow.

Stripped of clutter, the mind finds peace,
In moments of quiet, we release.
With gratitude, we pause and gaze,
At the beauty of life's intricate maze.

Voices of wisdom softly chime,
Reminding us of the rhythm of time.
Through reflections, we come to know,
The depth of our being, the strength to grow.

Embrace the truth that you find inside,
In clarity's light, there's nothing to hide.
With open hearts, let's dare to dream,
In reflections of clarity, we beam.

The Tapestry of Realization

Threads interwoven, colors entwined,
A tapestry rich, by fate defined.
Each moment stitched with purpose anew,
A story unfolds, vivid and true.

Patterns emerge from shadows of doubt,
In the fabric of life, the essence gets out.
Every choice a stitch, every tear a seam,
In the grand design, we learn to dream.

With open eyes, we start to see,
The beauty in chaos, the harmony.
Each thread a lesson, each knot a grace,
The tapestry woven, a sacred space.

Celebrate colors, embrace each hue,
For in every fiber, the self shines through.
In the dance of the loom, we find our fate,
In the tapestry woven, we create.

Realization blooms, a guiding light,
In the heart's canvas, hope takes flight.
Together we weave, hand in hand,
In the tapestry of life, we stand.

Awakening to the Unseen

In silence whispers a soft call,
The shadows dance, the night does fall.
With every breath, a world unfolds,
A tapestry of secrets, the heart beholds.

Beneath the stars, the veils grow thin,
Eyes wide open, I feel within.
Mysteries linger in the gentle breeze,
Awakened senses bring me to my knees.

Each moment sparks a vibrant hue,
Where dreams reside, the old feels new.
Beyond the seen, my spirit soars,
In every heartbeat, the universe pours.

A dance of light, where shadows play,
In the cracks of night, I find my way.
A journey deep, through realms unknown,
In the vastness of the unseen, I've grown.

From whispers soft to thunder loud,
I rise, I stand, I am unbowed.
Awakening brings both joy and pain,
In the unseen's grasp, I break the chain.

The Turning Point of Awareness

A thought erupts, a spark ignites,
In the depths of mind, the endless fights.
Each moment beckons, a choice to make,
Do I embrace, or do I break?

The echoes of doubt start to fade,
Clarity blooms where shadows played.
A breath of courage, the path reveals,
Through tangled woods, my spirit heals.

With open heart, I trust the flow,
Guided by whispers, I let go.
The turning point, a leap of faith,
In every challenge, I find my place.

The light within begins to shine,
A newfound vision, solely mine.
In unity, the world feels right,
A tapestry woven from day and night.

Awareness dances with every breath,
In living fully, I conquer death.
The turning point unfolds in grace,
With each new dawn, I find my space.

A Flicker of Understanding

In the quiet pause, a thought appears,
Glimmers of truth dissolve the fears.
A candle's glow, so soft, so clear,
In the shadows, I draw near.

Moments intertwine, a gentle sigh,
Wisdom blossoms, it cannot lie.
The flicker dances, a soulful song,
In the heart's rhythm, where I belong.

Each heartbeat whispers a tale to tell,
In the silence, I know it well.
A flicker of knowing, ignites the mind,
In every moment, the answers find.

Drawing close to the mystery's core,
With each revelation, I crave more.
The light that flickers, burns so bright,
Guiding me forward, into the night.

Embracing the grace of what I see,
In the flicker, I find the key.
Understanding flows like a gentle stream,
In the heart's chamber, I live the dream.

The Moment of Reckoning

In the stillness, a clock ticks loud,
The weight of choice, a shrouded cloud.
A moment comes, to stand or fall,
In the face of truth, I feel it all.

The echoes whisper of what's to be,
Reflection stares; will I be free?
In the mirror's gaze, I find my soul,
A fragment of light, a broken whole.

The moment strikes, the past collides,
With futures bright where hope abides.
Steps taken forward, or retreat in fright,
In the dawn of change, I seek the light.

Resilience stirs within my core,
In standing tall, I seek for more.
The reckoning calls, I face the storm,
In trials faced, my spirit's form.

Now here I am, no longer swayed,
By stories old, by fears portrayed.
The moment of reckoning, I embrace,
In its fire, I find my grace.

Milton Keynes UK
Ingram Content Group UK Ltd.
UKHW022119251124
451529UK00012B/603